Everything I Needed To Know

To Raise Children,

I Learned At The Office

Everything I Needed To Know To Raise Children, I Learned At The Office

A Parent's Guide To Growing Those Little Investments

REBECCA   SELINE

Illustration by Ingo Fast

iUniverse, Inc.
Bloomington

Everything I Needed To Know To Raise Children, I Learned At The Office
A Parent's Guide To Growing Those Little Investments

iUniverse books may be ordered through booksellers or by contacting:

iUniverse
1663 Liberty Drive
Bloomington, IN 47403
www.iuniverse.com
1-800-Authors (1-800-288-4677)

Because of the dynamic nature of the Internet, any web addresses or links contained in this book may have changed since publication and may no longer be valid. The views expressed in this work are solely those of the author and do not necessarily reflect the views of the publisher, and the publisher hereby disclaims any responsibility for them.

ISBN: 978-1-4620-6139-6 (sc)
ISBN: 978-1-4620-6147-1 (ebk)

Printed in the United States of America

iUniverse rev. date: 04/14/2012

Contents

Acknowledgments

To my daughters, Kyle and Erin, more love than you'll ever realize. To my husband, Rex, buckets overflowing with love and appreciation. To my parents, Wayne and Elizabeth Brugman, and siblings, Cindy, Wes and Steve, much appreciation for your unconditional love and dedication to the family. To Diane Asadorian Masters, thanks for more than 25 years of great friendship and fun. To other family members and friends, love and thanks for your inspiration and support.

In memory of Barbara Albright Westray.

Intro

Just As I Was Concentrating On Raising My Kids, My Mind Wandered

There I was, a heap of bone-tired mass spilling out onto the bathroom floor; my head resting on my arm on the edge of the bathtub, watching my two daughters, ages 3 and 5, bathe together. It seems so hard to imagine this now, more than 15 years later. They would no sooner bathe together now than wear the same color shirt on the same day. But back then, it was different . . .

The little one had just learned that the potty was there for a purpose and that she could use it — unlike the microwave, which was off limits. Having just learned the art of pottying, she would get into the bathtub, proclaim that she needed to use the potty and hop out, skip across the room (her path was carpeted), tinkle, then return to the tub; only to repeat this over and over. The very sight of that amount of water seemed to make her want to tinkle. I thought I might never let her bathe again.

Meanwhile, I needed to get the older one — who had been playing in the water and was now so wrinkled that it reminded me I needed to scrape off the raisins stuck to the kitchen chairs before their dad came home and sat down — out of the tub.

She turned to ask me why she had to get out first. Never one to say, "because I am your mother and I said so," I wracked my tired, drained brain for the actual reason. Why, indeed, other than the fact that she was clean, that her mother was about to melt into goo and that it was her bedtime, should she get out of the tub? Failing anything logical, I blurted out, "First in, first out," and then I giggled. Perhaps more commonly used when accounting stock sales or for inventory management, "first in, first out" seemed to work here. She popped out and the rest of the evening went smoothly (perhaps because I was feeling a bit lighter in my step due to cracking myself up with the new use of this term).

In fact, my mind kept dancing as I came up with terms that were used in the business world that had a completely different, yet often practical, use in the world of home and kids. So, as I carted my children off to swim and dance lessons, as I watched them practice soccer or as I waited for them in carpool lines, I entertained myself with this little game.

And now, after years of lessons and practices, carpool lines and graduation ceremonies, I am ready to deliver *Everything I Needed To Know To Raise Children, I Learned At The Office.*

The Job Of A Lifetime . . . *The Job For A Lifetime*

Wanted:

Full-time employee to work for a younger boss. Must be able to handle screaming, yelling and, sometimes, kicking and hitting. Must be able to lift increasingly heavy objects. Needs to be available 24 hours a day, 365 days a year. Much overtime, including weekends and, especially, holidays. Couple welcome. Specialists need not apply, generalists only. Experience helpful but not necessary. On-the-job training available. Several degrees required. (Advanced degrees of patience, compassion, love and understanding — just to start). Must be comfortable enforcing the D word (discipline).

No pay for this position — in fact, substantial investment required. *Benefits vary.*

Parenthood is a complex, diverse, wonderfully fulfilling and dynamic job — for a lifetime. What other job can offer that? And yet, considering what's involved, it's a wonder people continue to procreate. Even before the baby's first "waaa," the parents' lives are forever changed. For one thing, children broaden your horizons (and hips). Who used to think about what goes into baby food? Who used to think about what happens to disposable diapers after they leave your house? (I have to admit, I tried hard *not* to think about that. Once it was dirty, my main thought was when the next garbage pick-up was scheduled.)

After babies, your values shift. You used to think it important to arrive at destinations looking fresh and clean. Give a child a hug, and that starched and pressed shirt becomes as attractive as a used tissue (especially after the little one has been eating oatmeal or chocolate pudding).

After children, just getting out of the house is the goal. Who cares how you look? Besides, who said that shoes or socks had to match? In fact, after children, this can be seen as a status symbol — owning more than one pair, I mean.

Additionally, what you invest in changes. Can you say diaper futures? Generally, you just plain look at everything differently, including business issues.

For example, ask a newly pregnant and expanding woman about belt tightening. Then, check in with her at seven months pregnant and beyond and you'll find that rollovers have nothing to do with IRAs. And speak to her husband — who often wishes she could (rollover) without his help, and that of the two cats and the dog. Later, consult a mom who recently delivered a child about the ease of downsizing.

With children on the scene, many families instantly go from a for-profit organization to a not-for-profit disorganization.

The dinner hour turns into the dinner two hours — or the dinner five minutes. A simple evening out for two can turn into a logistical nightmare. And family outings require much more than a wallet and keys to the car.

Yet, those little subsidiaries, even if they merely drain the bottom line, are a valuable asset. They have substantial intrinsic value. But their development isn't always easy. Their trend lines change all the time. Historical comparisons are not always accurate.

And, if keeping up with product development (raising the kids) is not enough to fill 36 hours a day, toss in obligations outside the family for truly overbooked calendars and overloaded brains.

No matter our circumstances, at times we all feel conflicted between our family and other commitments. We all long for balance and simplification — and a little bit of fun.

Finding ways to combine our worlds might just be the ticket. In fact, what about bringing home some terms and phrases from the business world and using them in domestic and child-rearing situations? Hmmm . . .

Terminology For The Growth And Development Of Your Little Investments

Definitions

A-B

Absolute Advantage. Good genes. We all know people like this. They effortlessly produce beautiful, well-mannered, smart, athletic, musical children. They never break a sweat and they don't even have worry lines. Their kids' bangs are never in their eyes and their shoe laces never come untied, except when it serves to perfect the cute image. And, of course, instead of everyone hating them for their perfection, they seem to draw admirers by the dozen.

Accelerated Depreciation. What pregnancy and childbirth does to a woman's body: stretch marks, varicose veins, expanded hips and the dreaded droopy breasts. Sure, a woman's value and self-esteem should never be determined by her looks, and gravity is a fact of life. But pregnancy does have a tendency to speed things up (actually, speed up things falling down).

Accounting Errors. The onset of amnesia when your spouse asks you how much your recent purchase cost. Most often, the price is drastically deflated, but, unfortunately, so is the bank account.

Activity Charge. The cost to participate. No matter if it is chess club, tennis lessons, church committees or local charities, the minute you sign your name, the charges start pouring in. Clothes, shoes, equipment, extra training, transportation and take-out meals eaten on the run because schedules overlap — it all adds up. It's a lot cheaper just to sit at home. — The cost of being part of something worthwhile, well, it's expensive.

Advance Decliners. Mid-term notice that a child's grades are slipping. This early notification is sent home by a teacher so that if quick action (hopefully, by the student, not the parents) is taken, the decline will be reversed before report cards at term's end.

Amortization of Fixed Assets. Method of justifying the deluxe crib, extra-special stroller and to-die-for changing table and rocking chair. The cost of these deluxe models can be hard to justify if used for just the first few months of a child's life. However, if you think about using them for another child, the cost is easier to justify. Two or more additional children and, suddenly, the budget doors swing wide open.

Annual Report. That letter sent to stakeholders — family, friends and, sometimes, strangers — around year-end offering management's view of the family enterprise's past year. If public relations has anything to do with it, junior's bedwetting problem becomes, "Johnny is a very sound sleeper." Photos of key players are often included. Only younger executives (children) are featured if the senior executives (parents) are sensitive to how the past year has aged them. Key expenditures and capital expenses, such as new homes and cars, are common fodder. Big-ticket items must be disclosed (fancy vacations and second homes, new pets and other family additions). Executive departures (divorces) and the sale or spin-off of subsidiaries (children joining cults or communes) are often addressed in footnotes. The accountants often keep information brief, but marketing wants to list every ribbon and trophy earned all year. The SEC asserts no oversight, so while some hit the post office the Monday after Thanksgiving, others are lucky to reach their destinations by Valentine's Day.

Arbitration. What many fathers go through before a game of golf. When traditional negotiation between spouses (begging) fails, a third party enters the process, proposing alternatives: "Okay, if you let Frank play 18 holes on Saturday, he has agreed that you may go out to spend time as you please with no childcare duties all day Sunday. And there will be no questions about your expense report for the day. Sign here." A word of caution: The husband's golf partner may not be an unbiased arbiter.

Asset Allocation. Deciding what activities each child gets to participate in. Soccer, baseball, basketball, ballet, tap, jazz, karate, piano, violin, Brownies, Cub Scouts, origami — and those are just Tuesday's events. Everyone can't do everything. As a rule of thumb, each subsidiary needs to be in two places at once, but most parents can only handle needing to be three places at once. Multiple subsidiaries may require logistical support. (See **Pooling of Assets** for solutions to over-allocating your assets.)

Automated Teller. Most school classes, and many families, have at least one. To some kids, it just comes naturally. "Johnny pushed me." "Chloe copied." "Emily spit."

B-to-B. Baby-to-baby communication. For example, "Okay, let's really make the adults go crazy. Once I start crying, just give me a few screams, then you start in too. — Pass it on."

B-to-B Results. Comparison of your child's grades quarter-to-quarter. If it's B to B, fine. If it's A to A, great. But, if it is B to C, not so good. And if it's B to D, say goodbye to the cell phone.

Balanced Budget. When you run out of spaghetti and sauce at the same time. — Hopefully everyone has eaten.

Balanced Funds. Depositing equal amounts of money into your children's college accounts, no matter that one wants to go to college forever and the other is thinking technical school.

Balanced Growth. When a child outgrows everything at once and needs new shoes, pants, shirts, jackets, pajamas and underwear — all at the same time. While balanced growth means more cash outlay at one time, everything is new at the same time. The child looks fresh for at least a day. Unbalanced growth just means more shopping and something always looks worn.

Balance Sheet. What siblings mentally keep on each other. "Mom, you gave Sammy four cookies yesterday in his lunch, and me only three." "Dad, you always let Mona watch more TV than me." "Why does Teddy always get better birthday gifts than me?"

Barter. What you must do when you're in the park, at a birthday party or other gathering for children and you've run out of any of the myriad of items needed for a youngster. "Could I trade you this travel pack of baby wipes for a diaper?" You might even need to volunteer, "What if I toss in this health bar for you?"

Benchmark. The mark on the wall, the hole in the cabinet door and the nick in the dining room table — all made by children trying to retrieve something or trying an aerobatics stunt. "We're so proud of all of our children's benchmarks," could be the response defending why the disfigurations are still around, long after the children aren't.

Benefit Theory of Taxation. Everybody (almost) wins with this revenue builder. A child leaves something lying around. A parent picks it up. The kid, eventually, realizes it's missing from that spot on the floor and asks if anyone has it. The parent volunteers that the item, indeed, is in custody. The kid wants it back. The parent says, "Okay, for a price." The kid coughs up the money for the item. The kid learns you have to pay to have someone clean up after you. The parent gets back the money given to the child for allowance, which, by the way, was the last of the cash in the house. Everyone wins. Except the kid, in a way. Although he has his shoes back, he can't afford to go anywhere.

Best Practices. Usually happens when kids are well-fed, well-rested and actually want to participate in the particular sport/activity they are supposed to practice. Kicks are harder, throws are farther and music scales smoother when basic needs are met and the desire is there. But, just like what is said of publicity, bad practices are better than no practices at all. So, you just keep the kids running, hitting the ball, dancing or playing the music, even when circumstances aren't perfect.

Blanket Policy. Rule outlining where and when a comfy can be carried. A sample rule: A favorite comfy may be carried by a baby through 2 years of age on all occasions. However, following the third birthday, the blanky must skip all outings. Of course, every family can have its own rules, and often substitute items are permitted, such as stuffed animals or other small toys. In fact, many adults still carry around their own form of security blankets. (Can you say BlackBerry, iPhone, Android?)

Blocked Account. When a parent restricts the purchasing power of a child. There was one mother who had her chubby little son's picture posted behind the counter at the neighborhood store and asked the clerks to refuse him if he came in to buy candy. I bet he grew up and moved to Hershey, Pennsylvania.

Bluetooth. Usually accompanied by blue lips, blue tongue and, sometimes, blue fingers. Can be the result of eating a large portion of blue candy, frosting or popsicles. Actually, not as unsightly as purple tooth — often the result of too many grape-flavored treats.

Blue Chip. We all know families like this. They have been around for a while. The parents know the ins and outs of maneuvering their children's lives. The kids are always on the best athletic teams, they get the best teachers, and they know how to get a Pinewood Derby car carved and able to cross the finish line first.

Bond (high-yield). That irreplaceable, indescribable closeness and warmth parents have toward their children. It comes most frequently after a difficult day and the parents check in on a sleeping child, peaceful and sweet.

Bond (high-risk). That ultimate closeness that comes between two fingers — and, even more high risk, between a finger and lip — after a child has been playing in the Crazy Glue.

Book Value. Information provided by the librarian when your child has lost a library book and you need to know the cost to replace it.

Bottom Line. What you see when the diaper slips, revealing too many assets. Diaper weight and belly circumference factor into the equation.

Brand Extension. Mates, spouses or spouse equivalents brought home by children; can even include grandchildren. Sometimes brand extensions make you more fond of the original. (Remember New Coke versus original Coke, later termed Classic Coke?) In the case of grandchildren, the brand extension may be preferred to the original.

Budget. Managing what's going in and what's coming out. For example, it is Sunday evening and you only have a couple of diapers left. No one wants to go out and buy more. Careful planning and coordination of feedings, bathing and changing is required to make sure those two remaining diapers last until morning. And you just pray that the child does not develop any digestive problems during the night.

Budget Deficit. Snack shortage for the team. You've carefully counted the number of kids on the soccer team, have purchased snacks accordingly, even a couple extras for good measure. However, during the game, someone's siblings sneak in and grab several, unbeknownst to you. Bad news for the team. But good sports all, they share.

Budget Surplus. You finally get the hang of it. You purchase diapers in huge quantities for cost savings and to avoid running out at inopportune times. However, now your child is growing so fast that the dozens warehoused in the garage no longer fit. Oops. Can you say Craigslist?

Bull Market. When all conditions come together to give parents a euphoric feeling. The baby is fed, bathed, has clean diapers and is peacefully asleep. All is right with the world. This is when the child's stock with the parents is at its highest. However, as with all bull markets, the situation does not last. The child awakens. And various conditions — like how long the child has been asleep, how long the parents have been asleep (and, maybe what the child has interrupted) — determine how bearish the atmosphere becomes.

A **Bull Market** of another sort exists when you have to listen to a parent drone on and on about their child's accomplishments (real and imagined).

Burn Rate. The ratio of dinners that are edible compared with those that are so overcooked (burned) that they must be thrown away and new dinners delivered.

Bust. Returning home because the proper planning for the outing was not done. The children haven't had naps, the pacifier is lost and you don't have an extra, the favorite toy is in the crib, no snacks or juice boxes, the bottle is on the counter at home. There are countless reasons why careful planning and execution must take place whenever attempting to leave home with small children.

Buy-Back. Taking your husband's old clothes to Goodwill and then having to go buy them back when he discovers what you have done.

Buy-Back Agreement. When you learn. You now make a pact with the people at Goodwill that if you come back within 24 hours, you'll get your donations back, without having to buy them. Also known as a **Re-Purchase Agreement**.

Buy Long. The only smart practice when buying children's pants. Children outgrow long pants so quickly, and once the washer and dryer have their say, long pants can become awkward capris way too soon. *Antonym*: **Buying Short.** This can be an expensive lesson.

Business Principles Apply For 2ⁿᵈ Graders, Too

One day a friend of mine picked up her son at his new elementary school. The family was new to the community and had found spots in a highly sought-after school district for their two sons. Of course, the parents were worried that the kids would find friends and be successful. My friend was also concerned that she, too, would be accepted by the close-knit group of parents.

Well, on this particular day, it looked as if the happy ending was not to be. Her oldest son got into the car and said that he'd gotten in trouble at school that day and he had a note to show his parents. The teacher reported that my friend's son had responded to some words on the playground by shoving the girl that had called him names, and he followed that up with a note to the girl calling her some less-than-flattering names. His note also said that if she didn't cut it out, he was going to wait for her after school and shove her again. Apparently, when asked about it by the teacher, the son talked back saying his actions were justified based on the words from the girl on the playground.

Sensing that their happiness in the new community was at stake, my friend immediately called her husband and said he needed to come home right away. He questioned what could be so important that it would draw him away from his new job, where he, too, was trying to be sure his spot was secure.

"Just come home," she pleaded. "I don't know what to do." He rushed home and was a little dismayed that his involvement couldn't have waited another couple of hours. But, since he was home, he set out to teach his son the necessary lessons.

"Son, what have we talked about before?"

"That I'm not supposed to shove or hit the other kids?"

"Well sure, but that's not really the point."

"That I'm not supposed to talk back to the teacher?"

"Well sure, you're not supposed to do that. But that's not the big lesson here either."

"Dad, I'm sorry. I just don't know what else I did wrong."

"Son, now this is important. Are you listening?" The dad pleaded, as he envisioned lawsuits involving 2nd graders and beyond. "Will you promise to remember my words from this night on?"

"Sure dad," the son replied as he leaned forward for the message.

"Son, if you are going to call people names and threaten them, don't, and I repeat don't, EVER do it in writing."

Definitions

C-D

Cafeteria Benefit Programs. Anytime there is an organized effort to provide a selection of food for your child, thus saving you from trying to pull together a healthy meal or snack from the crumbs in your cupboards and refrigerator. While convenience, cost and variety are among the benefits, tastiness usually isn't.

Capitalization. This is one skill that comes pretty easily to kids. In fact, many kids start out spelling their names with all caps. It's the periods, commas and spelling that can be harder to master.

Carryover Charge. That friend of your child who comes to your home after school, stays for dinner, and then ends up spending the night. That carryover charge should be dropped (off at home) if it is still around after a couple of days.

Carpool Tunnel Syndrome. Inability to move in one direction or the other without feeling the pain — of bumping into another car. It is brought on by the repeated stress of waiting in a line of cars to pick up children from school and other activities. The stress comes from not being able to move to the left, right or backward; and only very slowly, forward. The condition is compounded if you need to be somewhere else at that very time or if you spot the PTA volunteer chair coming straight for your car. Nowhere to turn, nowhere to hide. You just know you'll be "volunteering" for something very soon. Stuck in the carpool tunnel. A bonafide condition, yet many insurance plans do not cover Carpool Tunnel Syndrome.

Cash. What our children have taken from us. Even before they can walk or talk — why, even before they were born — our children have a way of depleting our discretionary income.

Central Bank. Mom's checking account. This is where all major decisions regarding monetary distribution and spending are made. Interest in mom's checking account is usually very high.

Chain of Command. Ever see those people who put leashes on their toddlers?

Collective Bargaining. All the children in carpool joining together to try to get the driver to stop for ice cream on the way home from school. Lots of promises about homework are usually made.

Commerce. The ability of manufacturers to take nearly every baby item and make just enough changes so that the old item becomes outdated before the baby outgrows the need for it. Can really put a hole in the amortization of fixed assets theory.

Commodity. Babysitters. They often go to the highest bidder, and the good ones are rare. Try to beat the competition on pay. And keep great snacks on hand. Excellent snacks can go a long way in making up for misbehaving children.

Common Stock. As opposed to preferred or uncommon stock. My children are definitely preferred stock, I state modestly. And I hope everyone thinks their children are preferred stock.

Company. Anyone you clean the bathroom for. Also known as guests.

Company Policy. A set of rules outlining how children are to behave when guests are in the house.

Conference Call. When the kids are scattered all over the house and you stand in one spot and yell so that everyone can hear you at once. "It's time to eat." "Where is the TV remote?" "Who charged $214 on iTunes?"

Concession. Giving in to snacks and beverages at movies, sport events and concerts — often at a concession stand.

Conglomerate. Diversified family formed through mergers. When the merger first occurs, the primary focus can be temporarily lost. It can be difficult to determine who is in charge. Power struggles can occur, and lines of reporting can be blurred. Given time, most get back to their core concentration, gain a unified vision, clarify reporting lines, and various operating units coexist peacefully. If not, well then, most often they just spin off.

Consumption Tax. The price you pay for eating the leftovers on your child's plate. Yes, you are doing the world a favor by not letting the food go to waste. But there is no free lunch. And the price you pay is that those calories go right to the middle class: the hips and thighs. The tax assessor is not fooled by the usual dodge, "Mommy, you gave me too much ice cream again." "Oh, that's okay, just eat what you can." Then you swarm like a vulture after the child has left the table.

Contract Labor. Surrogate mother giving birth.

Cooking the Books. The outcome of inadvertently placing a cookbook or backpack on a hot burner on the stove.

Cooling-Off Periods. Also known as time-outs. We all need time to think things over sometimes. So, when your child responds with, "I'm too old for a time-out," you can counter with, "No one's too old for time-outs" — as you consider the fate of several well-known citizens who were given varying lengths of cooling-off periods — in the cooler, in fact. (Not recommended at home.)

Copier. The child that seems incapable of having an original thought. One who is constantly duplicating the actions of others.

Copyright. If you're going to duplicate someone else's work, you might as well do it error free, and then give them credit. "If you're going to copy, copy right," my neighbor likes to say.

Corporate Downsizing. When, despite your best intentions and efforts, those extra pounds just aren't coming off and you employ the resources of such huge entities as Weight Watchers or Jenny Craig to help you trim down.

Cost of Distribution. Time and money required to get the kids to all their activities.

Coverage Ratios. Percentage of clothing versus bare skin revealed when leaving the house. And, yes, face and hands do count in the bare skin portion. We favor high coverage ratios at our house. (At least I do.)

Credit. Self-esteem builder. Letting your children know just how important their actions are. "You set a good example for the rest of the kids." "If it weren't for you, the whole family would have overslept today." "You saved the game." However, problems arise when too much credit is extended. "Did you see how I showed everybody on the team how they should be playing their positions?"

Also, a promise of payment. My thoughts are that I am raising these kids and the only payment I'll ever receive is an empty house and time on my hands. Hmmm.

Credit Crunch. Ties in closely with **Credit Rating**. If a friend asks for a favor, you may quickly conduct a credit rating by calculating how many times you've been called to do favors for the friend. If you've been called upon a few too many times, a credit crunch can occur.

Credit Union. Group of parents that trade off caring for the other people's children. You borrow someone else's time to care for your child, you pay back by caring for their child(ren). Interest rates come into play. Once my kids were potty trained, I was way less interested in caring for children that didn't have proper appreciation for the bathroom facilities.

Cross Elasticity. The correlation between the loss of elasticity in a woman's stomach muscles and skin, and her general state of well-being. A woman can become chronically irritable (cross), if that area of the body decides to take a relaxed, extended vacation south.

Crude Realities. Facts of life after conception. Where do I start? Sex life taking a backseat to new life. Swollen breasts and ankles. Nervous daddies. Baby poop getting stuck under your fingernails when changing messy diapers. (Definitely hard to retrieve.) Junior-high-aged children ignoring the can of deodorant, bottle of shampoo, toothbrush or toothpaste they were issued. These children must be reminded to use them. Every day. Need I go on? Afterall, sometimes it's best not to know how reality will hit you.

Cyclical Employment. Parenting is certainly this. Sometimes it seems as if we are merely going around in circles, not making any progress. But, really, we are moving forward. And yet, the role of the school-age parent is seasonal. During the winter, spring and fall, the job is mainly that of chauffeur. During the summer, add entertainment director.

Day Trading. A somewhat risky strategy intended to take advantage of short-term scheduling swings. "If you take my kids all day Saturday so my husband and I can go to my cousin's wedding, we'll take your kids next weekend."

Defined Benefit. Giving children a reason why they should do something instead of just issuing the instruction. "If you don't brush your teeth, they will fall out," as opposed to "Go brush your teeth."

You've got to think this one through though. Your credibility will suffer if you've threatened that teeth will fall out if they aren't brushed. Then after diligently brushing their baby teeth, they fall out one by one. When the permanent ones start coming in, the kid says, "Why brush? I brushed the other ones night and day, and they fell out."

Delayed Opening. When, due to scheduling conflicts, a birthday must be celebrated a few days after the actual birth date. Not only do you have to wait to find out what's in those tempting packages, but you also have to wait to eat the cake. I hate that.

Demand. What happens when you get on the phone. Everything is peaceful, all needs seem to be met and, at last, a chance to take care of some of the calls that need to be made. Then, out of the blue, "Mommy, take me to the potty." "Mommy, Janie just punched me in the eye." "Mommy, I think I'm going to throw up." Yeah, you're not the only one.

Demographics and Economics. An easy theory to learn. As the demographics of your family grow, your economics diminish. It is hard to believe as you are purchasing all those things for a newborn that there will ever be a more expensive time of life for the child. Can you say orthodontia? Band instruments? Summer camp? Sport shoes alone can really put you back a few.

Demolition Clause. "Should you choose to kick over your brother's Lego creation . . ."

Depository. That spot just inside the door where everything is dropped. Backpacks, lunch bags, briefcases, shoes and coats. Family members tend to think this is a very safe deposit, as it is the first place they look when trying to retrieve something. If something has, by some miracle, been put away — it can't be found!

Depression. A fact of life after you have children. You're depressed because your child is growing up. Or you're depressed because your child isn't growing up. You're depressed because your child doesn't play sports. Or, you're depressed because all your child ever does is play sports. What a rollercoaster.

Deviation. Veering from an established standard. Families, schools and other institutions encourage varying degrees of creativity and expression. Some let the participants go wild, while others go to all lengths to stifle it, to ensure everyone sticks close to a determined mode of thinking and behaving. **Standard Deviation** is the accepted amount of variance at a particular place. For example, some families wouldn't blink an eye at copious piercing, but wouldn't allow even a trace of alcohol at the home. For others, the exact opposite is true. Some families don't care if a child eats pretzels for breakfast, while others insist on "breakfast" food, no matter what is in it.

Diminishing Returns. Sign of a good Christmas — with fewer gifts than last year needing to be returned or exchanged.

Direct Deposit. When potty training clicks. Faster, cleaner, cheaper. Eliminates the middleman. From the first diaper until the last, parents long for the day when their children will directly deposit. *Synonym*: **Potty Training**.

Discretionary Spending. Money spent on items of choice, rather than obligation (like the rent or mortgage). I have TONS of money to spend as I please. For instance, I get to decide what brand of milk to buy. No one in my family can even tell you if I buy 95%, 90% or 80% lean ground beef. That's a decision all my own. As for how much and what brand of laundry detergent to buy, no one in my family has a clue. That's my call. I'm free to spend as I please.

Disposable Income. Money spent on items that are almost immediately trashed — disposable diapers, baby wipes, paper towels, napkins in children's lunches (and sometimes the lunches themselves), gifts from mothers-in-law living in communes in Vermont: "Yes, that necklace made from aged cheese cubes is so versatile, and, my, how fragrant."

Dissavings. Taking money from your child's piggy bank. If a tree falls in a forest and no one hears, does it make a noise? If you take money from your child's piggy bank when he/she is not around, is that stealing? Even if you gave the child the money? Hint: If no one is home and the dog barks, does it make a noise? (The neighbors say yes.) Somebody always knows.

Diversification. A portfolio strategy. We all know families who have tried for diversification. Sometimes it happens; sometimes the portfolio stays the same. Even if diversification doesn't happen, no two stocks are the same, even if they are in the same sector. Each has its own highs and lows. Times of high performance and low performance. Each stock has to be taken on its own value, not always expected to perform like another, even if they seem to contain the same components.

Dividend. What gets you through. Dividends are not always predictable. However, certain market conditions almost certainly produce dividends. A trip for ice cream often produces dividends. Hugs, kisses, artwork designed with a parent in mind are all dividends.

Division of Labor. It may be 50/50 at conception — won't go there. Alas, division of labor is never again 50/50. — Won't go there either.

Double-Entry. When a child storms into a room or house, obviously in a very bad mood, and the parent asks that the child go out and come in again — exhibiting a more pleasant demeanor.

Downsizing. When you tire of wearing your maternity clothes (after all, the child has celebrated several birthdays) and you decide to diet and exercise to take off that baby weight. (See **Corporate Downsizing** when you can't do it on your own.)

Durable Goods. What new parents stock up on. Be it furniture or clothing, it's good to get things that can withstand sticky fingers, spilled food and dirt.

Dummy Invoice. Bill for child's tutoring. *(It's a joke.)*

Was This In The Job Description? Is This A Promotion?

Experts now say that most people will have several careers in their work lives. Parenting has had different career stops for generations. And, different skills sets must be employed for the several distinct jobs of parenthood:

Baby/Toddler Parent. This is an entry-level position and can be compared to boot camp. Generalist skills are a must. You will be on duty practically non-stop from sun-up until sun-up, especially the first few months. If you thrive on maintenance and routine and excel working in a fog of sleeplessness, you'll love this job. You must be prepared to pick up from the floor everything from soup to nuts (literally). Additionally, you'll be heavy into security. You'll be protecting your belongings from the toddler; you'll be protecting the toddler from your belongings. It is helpful to possess a working knowledge of major nursery rhymes to calm an agitated child. Another requirement is the ability to look at bowel movements analytically. (Can be learned on the job.) When the child is sick and you call the doctor for a diagnosis, among the many fact-finding questions the doctor inevitably asks is what the baby's stool looks like. This is one of the more unpleasant responsibilities of the entry-level position. However, it soon passes *(forgive me)* and you move on.

Youngster Parent. Education and training skills are a major requirement for this position. The child will absorb knowledge like a sponge and watch your behavior and register it as what is good and right. I admit that I may not have been the best influence at this stage. My historical knowledge leaves something to be desired. Besides, as we all know, timing is everything. For instance, the day one of my children asked me if there were any dinosaurs left on earth happened to be the day that I learned that the final two of my stay-at-home mom friends were going back to work outside the home. I just replied, "Well, there are a few of us left roaming around. But I don't really know any others personally." I realized what damage I had done when she brought home her test. She had answered the question, "Do dinosaurs still roam the earth?" with, "A few. They are practically extinct and they don't really roam the earth anymore. Mostly they just stay at home and play games on the computer."

Besides, at this stage, the kids are really into science fairs and science projects. I feel for my kids. I was just no good to them here. My idea of a groundbreaking science project was to take two brands of coffee makers and plug them in to see which one spewed tasty Joe first.

Teen Parent. This is a whole new ball game. Supervisory skills are put to the test at this level. There will, no doubt, be several attempted coups at this stage. The teenager is likely to go around management to reach objectives. Colleagues of the teens will play a major role in your teen's performance. It is important to hold tight to the reins of management and hope you'll reap the benefits in later years.

Emotions run as high as the volume around a teen. Loud conversations with parents and friends, high-volume music and sound effects from video and computer games often raise the noise level to unbearable points, even among the best of families. Therefore, ear plugs are recommended for everyone in the family while children are in this age category. No one will hear anything anyone else has to say, and tight bonds between family members will not be formed at this time. But the house will seem quiet.

And yet — as divergent as parents and teens seem at this point — it is important to remember that the two groups have many things in common. For example, each feels astronomical levels of frustration toward the other. This frustration can rear its ugly head in two questions that teens demand of their parents, and that parents demand of their teens — once again often in loud volume:

1. "WHY DOESN'T *ANYONE* EVER LISTEN TO *ME?*"

And,

2. "YOU'RE GOING TO *WEAR THAT?*"

Adult Child Parent. If you've played your cards right and have had your share of luck, you reach this stage at last. Just as your management responsibilities lessen, you realize that whatever the age, your child will always be your child. And even at this stage, when your offspring gets a toothache, you hurt. Hopefully, though, you won't have to pay the dentist bill — and that does ease the pain.

Definitions

E-F

Economic Efficiency. Signing one kid up for lessons, then bringing all the others to listen and observe. It is amazing what the tag-alongs can pick up if they'll just pay attention.

Economic Indicator. Most of us are dying to know the salaries and/or net worth of friends, colleagues and the parents of our children's friends. We look at their purchases for clues. Common comments include, "How can THEY afford that camp? How can THEY afford that school? How can THEY afford that house?" What we really mean is, "Why can't WE afford that camp, school, house?" (See **Income Statement** for more on this.)

Economic Planning. Preparations for costs that lie ahead, which must include disaster money: car problems, dental work, special tutoring and coaching, damages to neighbor's property by our kids, and, worse yet, damage to our own property by our kids.

Elastic Demand. When pants with set waistbands are just too confining and the need increases for flexible, stretchy waistbands. Do you really think all those people running around in yoga pants actually practice yoga? One woman that works as a consultant from home told me she makes herself put on clothes with a set waistband at least once a week, just as a belly check.

Electronic Caveat Emptor. The warning that should be applied to most electronic toys and games: "This electronic device can only be operated by a child." Isn't it amazing the things that children know how to operate almost instinctively? Lucky I'm not made of computer chips or my kids would know just how to get to me. They already know how to push most of my buttons.

Escalator Clause. An acquisition tactic. "We can ride the escalator if you are good while mommy looks at shoes. And we can ride it three or four times if you're good while mommy tries on shoes. And we'll spend the rest of the day riding that darn thing if you just give me enough time to buy some shoes I really like."

Escape Clause. It's just nice to know there is a way out. Hopefully you never have to use it, but sometimes it can be useful to let others know it exists. "I do have that friend in Hawaii who says I am always welcome . . ."

Even Lots. Twins, quadruplets, sextuplets.

Excess Capacity. Owning a car with more seat belts than family members. Having a home with more beds than family members. The problem with excess capacity arises when others find out and prevail upon you to constantly operate at full capacity: "Can you bring Bobby home from school?" "Is it okay if Josh spends the weekend at your house?"

Export. Child studying abroad.

Extraordinary Gain. A child coming into a family.

Fair Trade Law. Rules governing exchanges between children. Applied to cases when an older sibling tries to cut a deal. "I'll give you the pajamas with the feet in them for that new video game you bought with your allowance. You've already played it a lot anyway," offers an older sibling to a younger one. An adult needs to step in and referee. Intimidation by someone older should only be done by someone like, say, you. "If anyone gets that new video game, it's me."

Fee. What children automatically turn 365 days after their 2nd birthdays.

Fees. Not to fear, everyone says the fees are not as terrible as the twos.

FIFO. First in, first out. Rule applied when two or more children are bathing together and the time comes for removal from the bathtub. The unshakable logic of it serves to answer the inevitable question, "Why do I have to get out first?" It makes sense and keeps it all very simple.

Finders Fee. What mom or dad charges the kids for the return of items picked up that have been left all over the house. See **Benefit Theory of Taxation** for how this practice is helpful to *nearly* everyone in the family.

Fixed Assets. Sagging jaw lines lifted, noses reshaped and the enhancement of other portions of one's body. IM and texts are sent in record speed once someone gets word of another's recent asset fixing.

Also, often there comes a time in a man's life when he feels he has enough small children in his house. This may be when he decides to have his private assets fixed. Also see **Liquid Assets**.

Float. Refreshing treat traditionally involving root beer and vanilla ice cream.

Flow Chart. Diagram of a home's plumbing. It's always good to have a blueprint of the house's plumbing on hand. An emergency is no time to be running around trying to figure out where certain pipes lead, or, even more dangerous, just waiting to see where the leak in the upstairs shower will drip through.

Forced Savings. When the children find the bag that is going to the Goodwill filled with their old toys. Suddenly, the bag is empty and the closets overflowing again.

Forward-Looking Statement. Keeping both hands on the wheel, eyes steady on the road and maintaining appropriate speed while informing the children of their punishment for misbehaving in the back seat of the car.

Frozen Assets. What you are likely to get at some point if your child participates in an outdoor sport. Even in Southern climes, the weather doesn't always cooperate. And it can be very chilly sitting and watching others chase a ball. Frozen assets can also occur if your child receives a new bike during the months from November through March and needs help learning to ride.

Full Disclosure. When you tell your teen the complete truth of your youth. (See **Management Information System** when you choose not to tell it all and have to employ the help of others to keep it quiet.)

Futures Trading. What many parents do when they give in to a child's every whim. They are trading a peaceful present for a future with a whiny, spoiled adult child.

Ten Ways To Tell If Your Child Is A Good Investment

It's a good idea every now and then to take a look at where your money is going. If you have children, you'll notice that a lot of your money is spent for their well-being. And while most of us want it that way, occasionally, we might be tempted to see if our investment is paying off. Here are a few ways to measure:

1. **Prospects for growth appear strong.** When kids are small, this is easy. They grow physically and mentally every day. As they age, the changes are less apparent on a daily basis. But, as parents, we want them to continue to develop mentally and physically forever — at least in ways we approve. When they begin to venture into areas we're not so comfortable with, we long to reach out, bring them in close and sing softly in their ears the song that many crooners have recorded, "**You've** Gotta Be **Me. You've** Gotta Be **Me.** — What else can **you** be but what **I** am?"

2. **Exceeds expectations.** When a child exceeds your expectations, even just once in a while, why, that can carry you for some time. "Call the grandparents, Thomas tinkled in the potty today!" "Emma actually made her bed without being reminded!"

3. **Dividends come from investment.** The best dividend of all is, "I love you mommy," or, "You're the bestest, daddy."

4. **High PE ratios.** This is when the days a child actually participates in Phys Ed class outnumber days the child finds excuses to sit out.

5. **Has unique characteristics in the marketplace.** A given — what kid is just like any other?

6. **Keeps you abreast of emerging trends.** Who else to turn to to teach you how to obtain music from the computer, to tell you what's hot to wear (and, more likely, what's not), or to keep you abreast on the latest sports equipment and apparel (that they very likely desperately need)?

7. **Provides tax deduction.** And is so helpful in using up all discretionary income as well.

8. **Offers investment diversification.** Who knew baby formula was so expensive or that you'd end up spending more on your kids' shoes than on shoes for yourself?

9. **May some day spin-off, become independent and contribute back to the parent company.** Likely a welcome thought as you contemplate your senior years.

10. **None of the above. For you it's just an emotional hold.**

Definitions

G-H

General Obligation Bond. Social kiss or hug.

Glass Ceiling. No parent in his/her right mind would install one of these. Just keeping the windows and doors fingerprint-free is challenge enough.

Going Green. What's happening right now in the back of your refrigerator if you haven't thrown out last week's leftovers. Really. This time look *behind* the ketchup.

Golden Handcuffs. The hold that McDonald's has on parents. Children love the place. But is it the food or the toys?

Graveyard Shift. The duties assumed by the parent that happens to be at home when an animal dies. When a critter meets its maker, performing a eulogy is relatively easy compared with handling the deceased. That said, Sam the Goldfish is easy to flush. But the bird that crashed into the front picture window is a little messier.

Grace Period. The time between when you calmly ask your child to do something and the time you raise your voice with the instruction.

Gray Market. That difficult-to-locate pool of older women who are wonderful babysitters. There are a few out there that like to care for children and are very good at it. But you may have to go underground to tap into this gray market. Often there is no formal network and the good ones are rarely available. However, once you get connected, one can often lead you to another.

Gross Profit. The portion of income left over at the end of the month. So named because there really is no other way to describe it, other than *totally gross profit.* If there ever is any money left over at the end of the month, it usually just goes right back into the business.

Group Insurance. Parents coming together to decide whether their children get to participate in a certain activity, thus preventing the, "Well, Martha's parents are letting her."

Guaranteed Bond. The feeling you'll definitely get after a little one-on-one time with your child, like the closeness following a road trip with your child. The bond is even more secure if iPods, iPads and cellphones were out of battery power or forgotten at home.

Headhunter. What I became after my daughters played with their Barbie dolls. The heads of those dolls just seem to pop off, and, once off, they never stay back on. I also became a clothes stylist as I tried to find the clothes that, inevitably, came off during play. I spent a lot of time trying to find the heads, clothes and accessories. (*I* don't have that many accessories and I spent more time dressing those dolls than I did dressing myself.) But it just didn't seem right having all those headless, clothes-less, shapely dolls scattered about the house.

Hedge Funds. Money saved in a special account for the planting of a wall of shrubs separating your property from the neighbor's. Every time my neighbors hosted an outdoor party, allowing guests to litter all over our lawn and play music not acceptable to the ears of my young children, I added a couple of dollars to my slow-growing hedge fund. My hedge fund was in constant need of more greenery.

Hidden Assets. When you keep it a secret from the PTA at your child's school that you are a talented artist, a proven fundraiser or a former teacher with great tutoring skills.

Historical Comparisons. Discussing the characteristics and merits of your family members throughout the generations versus the characteristics and merits of your spouse's genetics. Then bringing your children's traits into the discussion to see if any patterns exist.

"I *knew* that nose came from your side of the family. No one in *my* family ever had a nose like that."

Holding Company. Some guests like to hold the baby and some don't. This term describes those that do. See **Private Company** for those who come to visit and prefer to coo from a distance.

Hostile Takeover. A 3- to 7-year-old grabbing back a toy that was absconded by another child.

Human Resources. Issuing an "all hands on deck" for a family work project like raking the yard or cleaning the garage and then only employing the two-legged workers. While pets are often willing, their efforts are not always the most productive. Besides, Fido might find some things in corners of the garage that you didn't even want to know were there.

What's Your Management . . . Er . . . Parenting Style?

Management and leadership — keys to effective parenting. Getting the underlings to do as you wish. Motivate. Invigorate. Berate. There are several styles.

Parenting By Objectives
I object to your leaving your toys on the floor.
I object to your putting your feet on the table.
I object to you charging gas for your friend's car on my credit card.

Parenting By Consensus
All right, the food has been on the table for nearly an hour. Is everyone ready to eat yet? Does everyone agree that the food is now cold and tasteless?

Parenting By Intimidation
If you don't do as I say, I'll tell your mother. Oh yeah, I am your mother. Well then.

Parenting By Walking Around
If I have to walk around your *(insert **obstacle** of choice* — backpack, shoes, basketball) on the *(insert **location** of choice* — front porch, hall steps, kitchen floor) one more time, I will *(insert **threat** of choice* — throw it away, put it away *[yeah right]*, run away).

One-Minute Parent
Okay, listen up. I have only a minute. Don't ever smoke or do drugs, or have sex until you're married. If you do, but please don't, protect yourself. Make sure your friends are good people first and cool second. Don't cheat, lie or steal. Okay. Any questions? No? Good. Now have a great day at preschool.

Definitions

I-K

Inappropriate Shredding. When you leave mail on the table, forgetting that your child is now mobile. You turn your back and then find the mail on the floor, wet with drool, all torn up. And that is even before the dog gets to it.

Income Statement. Some see a car, a house, a designer handbag as their income statement — their high income statement. But, a true statement includes the dollars coming in as well as those going out.

An **Incoming Statement** is the excuse your child tells you when arriving home after missing curfew. Sometimes the incoming statement is so ridiculous that all you can do is quickly send the child to bed so he/she will not see you break out in laughter. Other times, it is insulting that they think you'd fall for such an excuse. "Really? *Really?* Tell that to me again, this time speak very slowly and look me in the eye."

Inconspicuous Consumption. First, hiding your massive Girl Scout cookie purchase in the pantry. Then hiding in the pantry to eat from your stash.

Indirect Cost. When you don't pay upfront, but you end up paying eventually. You never really know what (or how) you'll end up paying when you ask your spouse to babysit, do yard work, or wash clothes when he/she would really rather be doing something else. There is no upfront money required and no money ever changes hands. But, trust me, you'll pay. You'll pay.

Inflation. What conversations with children sometimes contain. "There were a hundred million trillion ants on their driveway." "Everyone else is going." (Key word is everyone.) Exception: "You are the bestest mommy." No inflation there.

Insider Trading. Kids exchanging lunch items within the confines of the cafeteria. Their method of exchange is such that it usually goes undetected by authorities on duty. It has been proven that kids who have packed their own lunches tend to have the advantage in these trades over those kids whose parents packed their lunches.

Then, there was one young girl who didn't stand a chance the day her dad made her lunch. I was eating lunch in the school cafeteria with my daughter and noticed one of her friends taking a sleeve of soda crackers and a jar of peanut butter from her lunch bag. I asked her if that was what she usually brought for lunch. She replied, "Not at all. But my dad made my lunch today."

Interest (low). You have to be careful not to slip into this one, "Mom, can't you just pretend you're listening like you usually do?" *(Ouch.)*

Interest (high). When the teacher starts the conference by complimenting you on what a great kid you have.

Internal Audit. One last check that the milk is in the refrigerator instead of on the table, the iron is unplugged, the dog is in his place, and that all the children are in the car before leaving the house.

Investment Analyst. Your child's teachers. They can see into your child like few others. They compare your little investment to others in its class. They often point out the positive and negative characteristics of your child. They have the statistical information to compare past performance and, then, use it to predict future performance. They may recommend if you should hold this investment (back a year). They try to keep a perspective on the short-term gains, while keeping their eyes on the long-term prospects.

Rarely does the investment analyst ever recommend divesting your little asset, no matter how poor the performance. Usually additional investment is recommended (either of time or money in the form of tutoring).

Investment Cycle. Spend a lot of money before the baby is born, spend a lot of money on the baby, spend a lot of money on the toddler, spend a lot of money on the youthful child, spend a lot of money on the teen, spend a lot of money on the adult child or grandchildren. The investment cycle of a child remains constant, and never ending.

Junk Bond. When you or your children form a close relationship with fried, fatty and, generally, unhealthy foods.

Kickback. If first you get kicked in the cafeteria or on the playground, everybody knows you have to kick back. Then run to tell the teacher you got kicked.

Do They Teach This In B-School?

Strategies That Produce Results *(Although Maybe Not The Results You Were Expecting)*

Perception is reality. Always act as if there is no doubt in your mind that you know what you're doing. Act in control and you might actually convince yourself (and others) that you know what you're doing. While we all know the benefits of this around the office, don't leave the practice at your desk. Like bosses, kids smell fear and uncertainty. And like bosses, they pounce. And like some bosses, they kick, they scream, they plead. You must take control. Talk calmly, keep moving and distract. For example, your children start begging for candy and such things in the grocery store. Their whines turn into tantrums. You may wonder what to do: A) Just walk away from the cart — groceries, children and all — and go get in the car (very tempting). B) Start yelling at the children (what good would it do? They wouldn't hear you over their own screams). C) Start yelling for help (No use. Who would want to get involved in this mess?). Answer: D) Talk calmly, keep moving and distract. And on the way out, buy yourself some candy. You deserve it — having to deal with these children — who obviously aren't being raised properly.

Know your competition. It starts innocently enough. When a newborn is in your life, you just notice other babies more. You want to share with others going through a similar experience. You go up to strangers with babies and coo with the little ones. Then you ask how old the baby is. As your baby grows, you still go up to people. If your baby isn't sleeping through the night, you ask if that baby is. If you think your baby should be walking and isn't, you ask about that. At first, it is just finding common ground. Raising a brand new human being is awesome and it's fun to bring others in. Yet, over time, that competition (and, frequently, intimidation) thing sets in and the questions become more detailed. Soon, you're accosting other parents in such situations as preschool interviews with questions like, "And how many languages does your child speak?" Or, "Does your child play more than three instruments?" Next, you and your child (often unbeknownst to the child) are competing on levels previously never even dreamed of. For instance, on the day that the science projects are due, an elementary school-aged child is excited to be finished and eager to tell others about their project. The parents, on the other hand, are eyeing the other kids' projects, making mental notes for next time and tattling on kids that seem to have gone over budget, or, heaven forbid, have gotten parental help. Then you just look with pity upon the children who obviously did their own work or stayed within budget. They don't stand a chance.

Find common ground with your adversaries. It throws them off guard. The only way to truly excel is to get an angle. One of my daughters was so happy about losing her first tooth that she couldn't contain herself during the initial kick-off at a soccer game. She completely threw her competitors off guard by leaning across to ask an opposing team member if she'd lost any teeth yet. The fact that my daughter wasn't following the ball down field was irrelevant. She wouldn't have been doing that anyway. The fact that she had successfully prevented a member of the opposing team from doing so was ingenious.

Do not ignore the administrative. I have seen even the best business falter due to lack of attention to administrative tasks. And mark my word, in just a few years my children will be filing a lawsuit against me for lack of proper record keeping in their baby books. My children's contemporaries' baby books will be winning awards as coffee table decor and my children's won't even get a nod from the judges. As for my marriage, it has been teetering for years due to my lack of checking account-tracking skills.

Nothing stays the same. Prepare for change. Remember when phones had no memory? It used to be that people were smarter than their phones. Not that everyone was smart: It's just that phones knew nothing. Phones didn't talk, they had no idea what people's phone numbers were or who you last called, and they certainly wouldn't do your dirty work of dialing a desired number. Now, don't get me wrong, I like my phone knowing more than I do. I am just saying, it wasn't always that way and there is a period of adjustment. In fact, just as I get used to one phone, a new one comes out with more capabilities and I have to learn that one.

It was sort of the same when my children were growing up. For instance, I would put tremendous time and effort into figuring out the baby's "natural schedule." When she had her dirty diapers. How much sleep and exactly when it was needed. How much food she needed. And how much stimulation was appropriate for her developmental stage. And, just as I would figure it all out, arranging the entire family's schedule around the baby's, everything would change. Then, my research would start again, and the entire process would be repeated. So many adjustments. The kids continued to change on me every time I thought I had them all figured out. And, now that the kids are practically grown — well, I think this is the hardest adjustment of all.

Success does not last indefinitely. All those parents who were incredibly smug when their children walked at nine months are in hiding when those same children don't know their multiplication tables in the eighth grade. Besides, remember Enron, HealthSouth, WorldCom and the many other companies whose bright stars were forced to face the bright lights of interrogation?

Be nice to everyone. It's always the ones you were mean to that you end up needing the most. That snotty-nosed kid in preschool is now your child's lockermate. Or the mother of that snotty-nosed child is now the parent liaison on the committee deciding who gets which teacher for the coming year. You need her. You wished you'd let your child have a play date with her kid afterall. One friend of mine moving back to her small hometown to raise her family after living away for several years asked her mother, "How mean was I to everyone in town before I left?" "We'll find out," replied her mother.

It's the little things that get us through. Paydays, holidays, good reviews. Same with children. Paydays are when the child makes you an incredible birthday present, such as a hand print in Plaster of Paris (I'll keep that forever and reminisce about her early years), or when you have just lectured the misbehaving child on proper behavior and the child looks up a you with unbelievably innocent eyes and says, "I love you." Then those memory-making outings to the park, the heart-swelling birthdays and holidays spent together and the rare times when your teen turns to you and says, "I'm really proud of you." That's what makes you want to get up and do it again another day.

Don't take credit for other people's work. It's your kid that learned to read at four years old. Not you. Will you also take complete responsibility for your child's actions when he gets kicked off the basketball team in junior high for drinking alcohol on the bus? It's a team project. No one gets all the credit, or the blame.

Long-term views should be implemented. A small child is such a precious investment. But you need to have a long-term view. Check your investments daily, but never divest over one day's downturn. Evaluate every six months or so, and keep your eye on the future. Enjoy the dividends. I'll never forget the neighborhood kid that was so wild that even his parents wondered where he'd end up. But, he became one of the most dedicated, decorated law enforcement officers you'd ever want circling your block.

Reinvest the dividends. It strengthens the investment. All the positive stuff — hugs, smiles, handmade cards, bouquets of dandelions and other gifts from the heart — the best dividends ever distributed. Enjoy them and give them right back. They'll keep multiplying and pay off like no other investment.

Definitions

L-M

Labor. It just starts with childbirth.

Labor Agreement. Any agreement made between husband and wife during the birthing process. While not necessarily legally binding, these agreements are not to be taken lightly.

Example: Husband, "Come on honey, you can do it. You're doing great. Yes, yes, we'll go to the islands for the holidays. Yes, you can keep the nanny after the children are grown. Come on, you're doing great. No, don't stop now. We're almost there. Okay, you can spend a week of every month at a spa after the baby is born. And yes, I'll get up and bring the baby to you when it awakens during the night. That's it, that's it. We're almost there. Okay, okay, I'll fix breakfast every morning for the rest of our lives. There you go. Yes, we did it. Our baby . . . Whew, am I exhausted. I sure could use some sleep. I'm really looking forward to sleeping for about two days straight."

Wife, "Nurse, get my attorney on the phone."

Labor Force. Those family members who help with chores around the house. Some families have large labor forces, while others, even if they have several family members, may have a small labor force. Having a small work force either means a lot gets left undone or you pay others to clean your house, mow your yard or replace light bulbs.

Labor Slowdown. When the birth of a baby is progressing too fast and the doctor takes steps for a more relaxed pace.

Layoff. What you tell one child to do when he is teasing another child.

Lead Time. Usually about nine months. (Gestation period.)

Leading Indicators. Facial expressions and stride. When picking up children from school or another activity, it is telling how they approach the car. For instance, if the child is skipping or has the head up and is smiling, it is safe to guess that the day or activity went well. A child with a hanging head, a slow walk or shuffle and sad eyes is giving you every signal that some extra care is needed.

Level Playing Field. Doesn't exist. There is always a slant. What you learn through kids' sports, if you haven't learned it before, is that there is never a truly level field. Some kids are just months older, which can make a huge difference in ability at a young age. Sometimes the wind shifts just as your team takes the opposite side. Sometimes the umpire works for the other team's coach in his day job. You just go with it. Sometimes it works in your favor, sometimes not.

Liquid Assets. What a wanna-be father puts into the cup at a fertility clinic.

Liquidity. When a child has a liquidity problem, it is best to get right home. Most parents have had, at some time, the pleasure of seeing what went in their child's body come out on theirs (from one end or the other). However, it is not something you usually want to share — or, for that matter, something others want you to share. These liquidity problems frequently do occur in babies. And it is most important to keep the little ones hydrated.

Lock-Out. Once all the toys are off the floor, the house has been completely dusted and vacuumed, and the clothes are not only laundered but also put away, I consider locking the doors and not letting anyone in for a few days. But, this state of pristine living is usually extremely short-lived. I worry that everyone will find a place to live that they like better, so I let them back in.

Long-Term Forecast. While no one can ever predict what highs and lows may be experienced while raising a child, a safe bet is at least 18 years of little sleep. Additionally, heartache, pride, joy, fulfillment, optimism and a depth of love that can't be compared or fully described.

Loss Leader. The child that loses the most items in a given school year. Backpacks, sweaters, coats, and even pens and pencils. You'd think the kid was a magician the way things disappear.

Management Information System. Not telling your children everything about your youth, and getting others that knew you back then to also keep their mouths shut. *Antonym*: **Full Disclosure**.

Margin. When kids are toddlers, parents don't care where they color on a page. Most are just happy the writing is not on a wall. However, once kids start to school, this is one area of the paper that most teachers ask be kept clean.

Markdown. What you tell Mark to do when he is climbing on the counters. As everyone knows, when the "Mark down" doesn't work, the next step is the "right off." "Get RIGHT OFF that counter."

Market Analysis. Weighing the pros and cons of each potential grocery store in your area. Convenience, cost, whether it takes coupons, the likelihood it carries desired items and whether it houses a Starbucks are all valid criteria.

Market Correction. When you, your children and a store employee get down on your hands and knees to fix a **Market Crash** (see next definition).

Market Crash. Inevitable if you frequently grocery shop with children. Stacked items can only stay up for so long, and can take only so much bumping into. The sound of a hundred soup cans hitting the floor can be deafening. A few rolls of paper towels, not so bad.

When you try to explain your day to your spouse, talking about yet another market crash, don't be surprised with a response something like, "That's odd, the market was up about 10 points at lunch."

Market Failure. A very bad thing. When you're short on time, need a very specific item, and the store does not have it in stock. Or you need a specific item, are short on time, get the item in need, and once you are home and ready to use the item, you find out its "use buy" date has passed.

Market Turnaround. The grocery store dance. A popular step no matter if you've just run in to pick up a few quick items or have ventured up and down every aisle in the store at least once. The dance begins once you make it to the checkout line — that's where you remember what you forgot. The first part of the dance begins and almost looks as if you're nodding your head to the beat of some music. Actually, it's you looking back into the store to figure out where the forgotten item is located in relation to where you are standing. Then, you check to see how fast your line is moving. You do this a couple of times as you analyze how long it will take to fetch the item and get back in line to check out. Then, the full dance begins. You turn around, get out of line, dash to get the missing item and then hurry to get back in line. Market turnarounds are happening around the world every day.

Maturity. When a father lets the kids watch the TV programs they want instead of insisting they tune in to his. "Okay, the gist of your show is to cooperate with your friends, share and sing a lot. Now, let's tune in and see who's winning the game."

Means Test. One toy in a room with two children. See what means they use to decide who will play with it. Also shows how determined (mean) each of the children can get in order to play with the toy or get their own way.

Mental Pause. The time in a woman's life when she knows there is a reason she is so grumpy, but she just can't remember it.

Merger. Bringing together two families to make one. Also see **Conglomerate.**

Microeconomics. Concentrating on just one child at a time. *Antonym:* **Macroeconomics.** Considering entire family's concerns.

Mixed Economy. One spouse (working outside the home) eats on expense accounts or at business lunches. These are often lunches of adventurous, delicious food where the chef comes to the table to see if everything is satisfactory, and, most importantly, someone else does the cooking and cleaning. The only chef visiting the spouse eating at home is Chef Boyardee, and he doesn't check back to see if the food is liked or not. And he certainly isn't around for cleanup.

Model Year Variation. No two kids are alike. Even if they were built at the same factory, using basically the same parts.

Money Laundering. Part of the Monday morning routine. Don't bother calling the Feds. Most often there's not enough money in the dirty laundry to buy a Frappuccino grande.

Moonlighting. Required part of parenting, especially in the early years and then again in the teen years. Working dawn to dusk is not enough. Many times your services will be needed when you'll have only the moon and the heavens to guide your way.

Multi-Tasking. Holding a cup of coffee without a lid, fastening a seatbelt, singing the Barney song to placate a passenger, changing the

CD and keeping a two-ton vehicle under control while maneuvering a sharp turn at 35 miles per hour. Oh yeah, and spewing out a spelling word now and then to quiz another passenger.

Mutual Funds. Happens when the kids want a dog so badly that they offer to pool their own money to buy one. That mutual fund may really pay off in your senior years, when you need it the most. By then the kids are older and will no longer hang with you — but the dog will. That mutual fund was a good investment after all.

Choice Of Career Affects Child Rearing

Most of us, at some time while raising our children, wonder how others parent their children. And we're sure that everyone else is doing a much better job. Our children even tell us how wonderful other parents are: The proverbial "Susie's mom is letting her go" is declared in every household at some time or other, in some form or another. But a lot of things come into play that lead us to parent as we do. And there is no getting around it: No matter your chosen field, your career will influence how you parent. Take a simple school field trip to a science museum. What you want to hear about and the questions you ask reflect your point of view and, thus, very often, your career.

For instance, if you are:

An **Accountant**: "Okay, how many people left with you on the bus? How many returned? What was the total cost? How much did each student pay? Do you see this as a leisure or business trip? Do you have a receipt?"

A **Doctor**: "Did everyone feel okay? Was anyone running a fever? Anyone injured on the trip? No one got sick on the bus, did they? Had everyone had their immunizations? What do you mean the teacher couldn't read the permission note that I wrote for you?"

A **Rock Musician**: "You went where? Why? What kind of gig was there? Oh, you went by bus. Cool. We always go by bus. Any museum groupies? What did you do on the bus — play cards, listen to music, jam? What did you do for an encore? Was this just a one-gig deal or did you have other stops on your tour?"

A **Pilot**: "Did you leave on time? Return on time? Was there an equipment safety check prior to departure? Did everyone stay buckled while seated? No one operated any electronic devices while you were leaving the school did they? How about on re-approach?"

An **Administrative Assistant**: "Now let me take this down. You left at 10 a.m., arrived at 10:45 a.m., toured the museum until 11:30 a.m., ate lunch on the lawn and re-boarded the bus at noon. If you'll draft a thank-you to the bus driver and the museum tour guide, I'll type them up. Now, I see on your schedule that you have a math test third period tomorrow and a book report due on Friday. Is there anything else?"

A **News Reporter**: "Where did you go? Who went? What did you see? When did you go? How did you get there? How much did it cost the taxpayers?"

A **Lawyer**: "Did the bus have insurance? Were you properly chaperoned? Any suspicious characters lurking? Did you get hurt in any way? Did the bus stop quickly and jerk your neck at any time? Were the stairs at the museum clearly marked? Did everyone have equal access to the museum? Were all specimens you viewed at the museum equally represented?"

A **Politician**: "So, let's just say you enhanced your scientific knowledge today by visiting one of our nation's treasures. You went with your fellow students in an effort to build core-level support for better education in our schools and a broadening of experiences for children everywhere."

A **Real Estate Agent**: "So, did the museum make a good impression on you as you drove up? Were hedges trimmed, the building freshly painted? How about on the inside? Was it easy to find your way around? Everything nicely marked? Clean carpet? No animal odors? Did it seem like other people looking for a museum would find this one attractive, useful? Did it seem to have that move-right-in quality?"

A **Mom**: "Did you eat your lunch or did you just throw it away? What are those stains on your clothes? Did you go all day without tying your shoes? Why do you have bugs in your pockets? Did the other kids get this dirty? Do you have homework on this?"

Definitions

N-P

Net Gain. When your neighbor gives your child the soccer goal that his child has outgrown and the net is not torn or missing.

Net Investment. When that same neighbor gives your kid the soccer goal, but the net is torn and you need to buy a new one. — Those things are expensive!

No Visible Means of Support. You see it everywhere. Women dressed in clothing that no one can figure out how it stays put. Women — worth millions of dollars — with no visible means of support. Starlets on the red carpet have people all over the world at once asking, "How is that staying up?" And, more importantly, "Will it continue to?" It's an economics question that many like to ponder. Ah, the allure of mystery. Well, there is absolutely no mystery in **Visible Means of Support** when unsightly panty lines, bra straps and the like are all too apparent.

Options. Young children should have few of these. It is too confusing. They do not understand the concept and, inevitably, they choose the least favorite option of the parent. For instance, a parent that asks the kids where they would rather eat, listing a couple of restaurants, is just looking for trouble. Either each of the children involved will have a different opinion, or the kids will suggest going one place for part of the meal and the other spot for another part of the meal. Then they won't understand why you don't follow their lead. After all, you asked.

Organizational Chart. List of chores to be performed by each member of the household to keep the house in top working order. However, as in the business world, organizational charts rarely represent reality.

What happens when the person assigned to vacuuming can't do it because there is stuff on the floor and that picking up is someone else's job? The person in charge of taking out the trash is unable to perform responsibilities because there are no garbage bags and shopping is someone else's job. Besides, some kids are just better at dusting and some at cooking a meal. Sometimes you just have to work outside the lines.

Organized Labor. The satisfying scene of 3- and 4-year-olds putting away the toys before leaving preschool. Such a well-synchronized effort! Those same children rarely perform so well individually when putting things away at home.

Outside-the-Box Thinking. When someone is of the opinion that dirty clothes on the floor *next* to the hamper is acceptable.

Outstanding Balance. A credit card statement that shows a zero balance. In our family, this is a rare, but an OUTSTANDING BALANCE.

Overproduction. Is there such a thing as too many kids? How many is too many? Overproduction usually depends on the factory, management and product produced.

Pie Chart. The percentage of a pie (can be pizza or fruit) that can be consumed upon hearing disappointing or disturbing news. For example, child gets kicked off cheerleading squad for swearing at the coach — eat half of your favorite pie. Get speeding ticket while transporting the entire soccer team to a game — that's embarrassing — go ahead, eat the whole darn thing. Word of caution: Consult only one chart for consolation. For instance, the fruit pie chart should never be combined with the pizza consumption chart, no matter how bad things are. That is a potentially lethal combination.

Pooling of Assets. Signing up for carpool duty. See **Asset Allocation** for why.

PowerPoint. Words aren't even necessary. You just extend an index finger, directing it toward something and the child instinctively knows and obeys. For example, you point toward the bedroom, and the child knows it's bedtime. You point at the TV, and the child knows it must be turned off. You point to your favorite candy bar from their Halloween stash, and they automatically know to give it up.

Also very effective with the dog. One stern look and a power point will often get you your shoe or sock back.

Power Lunch. When the dog chews an electrical cord.

Preferred Provider. What people who marry for money call their chosen one. *Mary had many men offering to take her to dinner and buy her pretty things. In the end, she chose Steven as her preferred provider.*

Insurance companies often want to know our preferred providers of medical services. But for Mary, her preferred provider gave her an entirely different type of insurance.

Price Fixing. An automatic markdown. Altering an item's cost when telling spouse of purchase. See **Accounting Errors** for effects on checking account balance.

Prime Real Estate. Front and center at any activity your child is involved in.

Principles of Consolidation. What foods are and are not compatible, pertains especially to small children. It can be problematic to combine too many hot dogs with too much soda, ice cream and candy at a ball game.

Private Company. People who come to visit the new baby, but for various reasons do not want to hold the baby. See **Holding Company** for those that do.

Product Control. Early on it's careful watching, patient instruction, setting a good example. Later, it's curfews, grounding, surveillance.

Product Placement. Knowing to keep your organic carrot shampoo away from your cucumber face mask, or you'll have radishes growing from your forehead. — You almost need a degree in chemistry to pick from the thousands of products loaded with chemicals, herbs and potions designed to combat beauty deficits. It's a complicated equation. And, once you zero in on a product to buy, you still have to figure out where and how to use it.

Promotability. Something that at the end of every school year you hope your child has.

Psychic Income. Children may provide quite a drain on profits, but each year also provide more than their weight in gold in terms of pleasure and happiness.

Public Company. What your family automatically becomes the minute your child learns to put sentences together. Children tell anything and everything to your friends, their friends, teachers, even complete strangers. One preschool girl while en route on a field trip, pointed to a hotel and said, "That's where my daddy lives now." "Ohhhhh," was all that most of the surprised adults on the bus could muster as they shot looks of "I didn't know that," and "What should we say now?" to each other.

Put. Common instruction used by parents, teachers and other adults. Similar to **PowerPoint**, but words are needed for this. Involves the pointer finger and one common word, "Put." "Put that down." "Put your little behind here." "Put your shoes in the closet." Not to be confused with "Don't Put." As in, "Don't put that in your mouth." "Don't put your wet bath towels on the floor." And, "Don't put your bike behind my car in the driveway."

Pyramiding. Five kids in a gymnastics class. Five kids outside. Five kids in a schoolroom while the teacher slips out momentarily. In fact, whenever you have at least three kids together aged from about 2- to 8-years-old, you can count on them climbing on each other.

Enough Sitting Around, It's Back To *Real* Work (*Anything's Got To Be Easier Than This Full-Time Parenting Stuff*)

You'll know it's time to get back to work outside the home when . . .

- Precisely at 9 a.m. each weekday morning after getting yourself and everyone else in the house up and dressed, you line up your baby and all the stuffed toys around the changing table and announce, "Okay, today we need to accomplish . . ."
- You start arranging meetings with your friends to discuss budgets, current projects, long-term objectives, short-term objectives and marketing plans for your respective families instead of going for coffee, or taking trips to the mall, the zoo or to the park with the kids.
- You are constantly calling staff meetings and you have no staff.
- You find yourself spending extra time on your appearance the day you're to have your photo taken for your membership card to the discount shopping club. You really need to get out more. There should be bigger days in your life.
- You start talking to the appliances. Like when the dryer beeps to indicate that the laundry is dry and you walk over to it saying, "Okay, okay, I heard you. Do you really think you needed to beep twice?" Or when you walk over to the refrigerator to get lunch and as you open the door you ask, "Okay, what do you have for me today?" — as if it is the sandwich lady at the deli counter. Or perhaps when the oven overcooks your casserole and you respond with, "Aren't you a little hot today?"
- You are at a four-way stop and you always let all the others go first, no matter if you got to your corner first, thinking that they all have more important places to go than you. Or,

you're on your way to a function and you get out of your
car at a four-way stop to ask someone at one of the other
corners if your shoes go with your outfit. It's been so long
since you've gotten dressed up, and you just weren't sure if
you could trust the opinions of your 18-month old or the
grunge babysitter.

- You purposefully get in the longest line at the grocery store,
so desperate for adult conversation that you are hoping to
strike up a conversation with someone else in line — or at
least eavesdrop on someone else's adult conversation.

- When people ask you who you hang out with, you answer,
"Kelly Ripa, Kathie Lee and Hoda, and the ladies on 'The
View.'"

Isolation and loneliness are not your friends. It is really important
to get out of the house. Otherwise, you lose perspective on the
importance of things. What seems monumental to someone who
seldom leaves the house can be trivial to someone that gets out once
in a while. For instance, when someone once asked me what I did,
I said I was a stay-at-home mom. Well, I think I gave a little too
much information and lost perspective when I continued, "That
is except for today. Today, I went to the grocery store, the dry
cleaners and volunteered at the school library. But, most days, I am
a stay-at-home mom."

So if you decide to re-enter the workforce (outside the home),
there are a few things to keep in mind:

1. Adults do not take potty breaks nearly as often as children.
   If your bladder is now attuned to a 4-year-old's, limit your
   liquids before lengthy meetings.
2. Resist: "Sally, I can see you have on your sad face again
   today. Let me reach into my handbag. Yes, there it is. Let
   me help you put on your happy face, Sally. You'll feel much
   better."

3. At business luncheons, control yourself. As the waiter places soup in front of the person next to you, resist: "Careful, Fred, I think that soup is hot."

4. Or, "Fred, there is still some fish on your plate. Aren't you going to finish it? You'll be hungry before dinner. Okay, no M&Ms for you at our afternoon meeting."

5. And please resist the urge to nurture everyone: "June, here are some tissues to carry with you. That cold seems really bad and, forgive me (as you reach to feel her forehead), but you do feel feverish. I have some Ibuprofen (you say as you hand it to her). I really think it would help you feel better." And, "Didn't you bring a heavier coat today? It's supposed to get really cold. No hat? How about mittens?"

6. Remember your frame of reference. Count to 10, bite your tongue, stare at the ceiling — just don't automatically jump into a conversation that might have a context you are not aware of. For instance, one colleague says, "Wow, that is great. Brenda from accounting has been dry for 48 hours now." You (fresh from the diaper set), "Has she seen a doctor? In the group I'm used to hanging with, if anyone is still dry by mid-morning, we think they are not getting enough fluids."

Keep that parenting hat handy

You know you are not leaving the office at the office when you've had the children write out their six-month, annual and five-year objectives, and then you formally review their progress. "Honey, I noticed that on your last sheet of objectives you listed learning to ride your bike. I know that that has not been accomplished. If you need extra help, we'll see if it is in the family budget to bring in someone to help you. I really hate to see you fall behind on your plans. That probably means you have made no progress on learning to jump rope either. Am I right? Well, I'd like to hear of these things before they become problems. We'll try to get someone in to help bring you up to speed. By the way, I haven't seen a copy of your

budget for last month's allowance. How are we doing on that? I know you spent quite a bit this past week. We aren't over budget on sweets are we?"

Or, while other parents are making such comments regarding the new preschool teacher as, "Oh, we love her sweet voice." "I love her enthusiasm." "The kids relate so well to her." "She has such great bulletin boards and such an organized classroom."

You answer with, "We're cautiously optimistic. This first quarter has been going well. But, second quarter, near the holidays, that will be the true test. The ability to deal effectively with periods of heightened activity is telling." Then, after a pause, "Actually, it is awfully hard to speculate. Until yearend results are in, I really hate to comment."

Definitions

Q-R

Quota. Meeting an arbitrary standard doesn't apply to parenthood. After 2,500 diapers, you're going to quit? And there is no bonus system if you do more than the competition. For instance, there are no toaster ovens if you change more diapers than other moms or dads, and no free trips to the Bahamas for bathing your children more than the neighbors.

In parenting, you just do what you have to do. And if you don't — well, you just hope no one notices.

Random Noise. Ever been in a quiet place — church, an elevator or a meeting — and the child you're holding makes a socially unacceptable noise (passes gas, has a bowel movement, burps)? You just pray that the people around you realize that the baby made the noise, not you. Awkward silence or silly jokes usually follow. The situation is only made worse when you try to make excuses or explain what happened. Most of the time people already know what happened. They just don't want it to happen again.

Rank. How the tennis shoes of teenagers smell.

Rank and File. When you line up all the bills and place them in descending order of payment.

Real Income. "Now the Smiths, they make a REAL income." Whatever your household income, it is never enough. However, we all know someone's income that we think we could really live on.

Realized Loss. The expression on a child's face when she becomes aware that she left a soccer bag on the field or that an important book or report is nowhere to be found. It can be a heartbreaker for parents as well as the children. Hard lessons for the kids are usually harder on the parents.

Reasonable Accommodations. What I've been trying for years to achieve in our guest room.

Reciprocity. Mama said it best in the movie *Chicago*. "You do one for Mama, she'll do one for you." Throughout the years, many have learned, it pays to make Mama happy. She can do a lot for you — both helpful and not so. As they say, "It's good to be good to Mama."

Recovery. You never really get back to where you were before the baby. You just start from a new place.

Report of Operations. What conversations with your parents (and other relatives) can become. Uncle Jack had heart bypass surgery, Aunt Sue had a gall bladder operation, Cousin Tim has a new knee. And with the increasing number of "fix-it" medical procedures available, conversations with contemporaries can be filled with reports of operations as well — LASIK, rhinoplasty and other various nips, tucks and enhancement procedures.

Research and Development. "Johnny, go find out what kind of mood your mother is in. If she's in a good mood, ask if she wants to cook dinner. If she's grumpy, maybe we'd better go out."

Resting Order. Mandated nap time.

Retainer Fee. Should never be paid on a monthly basis. Most orthodontic treatment plans include the cost of one appliance to hold work in place once it's been completed. A monthly retainer fee means someone's being reckless. Johnny's left it on his tray in the school cafeteria and it got thrown away. Fido has decided to see how straight his teeth are. Or, maybe the retainer is still in the original container and being stored under a bed.

Return on Investment. Not to be confused with **Returns to Investor.** The former means the time you realize your child is a decent individual, who contributes back to society. The latter is the time you realize the child you thought was raised and living independently suddenly returns home and you must continue your investment.

Returns to Scale. Depends on the woman — when she decides to weigh herself following childbirth, that is. Some can't bear to do it for about five months. For others, it is the last stop on the way out of the hospital. Many then insist on another examination, sure that the doctor left another baby or a piece of heavy equipment inside her.

Revenue Recognition. Can be a power play. "Just remember who brings in the money here."

Rollover. Often extremely difficult for a pregnant woman to do on her own. While heavy machinery is rarely needed, it might be cause for all house personnel and pets to be on deck, poised for service.

Everything I Needed To Know To Survive The Workplace, I Learned Raising Children

1. **If something stinks, change it.** In the workplace, we tend to just get used to the smell. At home, that is impossible and unsanitary. If something's not right, we have to know when to break from the routine and change it. Because, just like a dirty diaper, if you don't get rid of the mess, it spreads. It spills over onto everything it comes in contact with and there's a lot bigger mess that, eventually, WILL have to be cleaned up.

2. **Just because you work the hardest and put in the most hours, doesn't mean you'll get paid the most.** I'll take anyone to the mat who says that stay-at-home parents don't have huge jobs. But that doesn't mean they are the highest paid. Usually they work for free. And if they got paid by the hour, well, very few families could even afford a stay-at-home parent. How many of us get overtime pay when we work extra to take care of sick children during the night, on weekends, and how about the holidays? Why stay? The Fridge benefits.

3. **Just because you're the smartest in the building, doesn't mean you'll get paid the most.** Hey, there are some days when I truly thought my 4-year-old and 2-year-old had one or two up on me. But then I'd really surprise myself and do something sort of intelligent. Like remembering to take out all the red T-shirts from the whites before putting the load into the washer. Or, I'd have all the soccer uniforms clean (and almost dry) before time to leave for the game. Nonetheless, the kids are the ones who really clean up on their birthdays. It's not that I'm bitter. I just wish they'd share.

4. **If you are being chased by a dog, don't run.** In most cases, you haven't done anything wrong; it is just the personality of the dog to go after somebody. If you just ignore the dog, or stand your ground, pretty soon the dog will get bored and go away.

5. **Sometimes you need to color outside the lines.** Sure, if you color inside the lines with the prescribed colors, you'll make a pretty picture. But it's likely to look pretty much like everyone else's. If you color outside the lines, using colors of your choosing, you make your own creation. The challenge is to know when it's best to do it someone else's way and when to break out and take a chance to create your own masterpiece.

6. **You have to know when to hold 'em and when to let 'em cry.** If you try to make everyone feel better all the time, without teaching them to calm themselves, you'll end up exhausted and everyone will be hysterical around you. Let 'em cry sometimes. They'll learn what it takes to calm themselves. You'll feel better, they'll feel more confident, and you'll be energized enough to help when there are real problems.

Definitions

S-T

Same-Day Return. What happens to those beautiful, wonderful, exotic, make-you-feel sexy shoes once you regain your senses and realize you no longer have anywhere to wear them. Chasing a toddler in them would be dangerous, walking the dog would be outrageous and wearing them for carpool would just be a waste. No, it's better to let them go to someone who truly needs them.

Service Economy. The principle we seem to employ at our house. "Mom, did you wash my jeans?" "Mom, can you take me to the mall?" "Mom, I left my iPod right here, where did you put it?"

Shortfall. When the climbing child falls from the kitchen counter rather than from the top of the refrigerator. That would be a long fall. See **Mark Down** for how to get your child off the counter.

Shuttle Service. That back and forth, back and forth that takes place nearly every meal between the table and the refrigerator, between the table and the microwave, between the table and the sofa in the living room. It is so exhausting that sometimes a nap is needed mid-meal.

Sock Market. The collection of socks gathered from the wash that went in with a mate and come out a single. Where do those mates wander off to? A singles sock bar? If the remaining single socks are not worn out, I try to find a suitable mate amongst the other single socks. Sometimes it is not as good of a match as the original. So, I have warned my husband not to put his feet too close together — to always keep them about a foot apart so that close comparisons can't be made.

Social Security. One of the benefits of being athletically gifted. It seems as if there is never a lack of people that want to be around successful athletes (and their parents). I don't know many football quarterbacks or their parents who sit at home on Saturday nights wondering what to do. Okay, I admit, I don't know many football quarterbacks (or their parents). But athletically gifted people, it seems, do enjoy a certain social advantage.

Another definition of **Social Security** is knowing that your best friend will be sitting right next to you in the cafeteria — every day. It's very comforting to have a pal who understands your secrets, no matter your age.

Specialization. No room in parenthood for this. "I really love babies." Well, do you have substitute parents lined up for ages 2 through 23? Or, "I don't really like babies. Once they reach school age, that's when they get fun." How about, "Diapers aren't really my thing!" Or, "I'm not really good at discipline." It shows! It is okay to hire specialists to fill in the gaps where needed. Just closely monitor those specialists and what gaps they might be filling!

Speculation. The amount of daydreaming and voicing of opinions surrounding babies is incredible. "Those long fingers — sure to be a pianist!" "Look at how long she is, a basketball career is in that kid's future." "Boy, that child comes up with the best stories — a writer for sure!"

It is amazing, then, that as children near adulthood, when you think those special talents and career paths would crystallize, the picture is often much fuzzier. How many parents (and children) are frantic with worry over the future of a 15- to 20-year-old? Where did all those optimistic predictions go?

Spin. Obviously — the last phase of the wash cycle on the machine. But also, what parents put on many conversations with their children. "Grandma didn't mean you are fat. You are just bigger than the last time she saw you." "Johnny didn't mean to kick the ball into the pit of your stomach that made you fall to the ground and puke. He just wanted to kick the ball near you so it would be easy to catch." "The teacher didn't mean that you are dumb. She just said that you learn differently . . ."

I imagine our children use a little spin with us, too. I don't even want to think about that.

Spin-Off. When a child decides to leave home and support himself/ herself.

Spin Out of Control. When a child decides to leave home and can't support himself/herself.

Stability. What every parent is overjoyed to see at every age. At first, it's getting a schedule down for the baby. Then for toddlers, it's surefootedness. For elementary kids, it's the ability to function and solve problems independently. Then as the kids age, it's finding a functioning, productive path for themselves.

Often, the primary challenge for parents as we watch our children's struggles and victories is remaining balanced and stable ourselves!

Standard of Living. Who would have ever guessed that you would put a huge, brightly colored plastic toy kitchen in your living room? Plastic plugs in electrical outlets, safety contraptions on all drawers and doors, and, suddenly, you have a new standard of living. Decorating style tends to be early toddler. Cupboards and pantries are so difficult even for adults to crack, that you wonder if it's really even worth going for that late night snack.

Standing Order. A little outdated method of discipline, but it can still be effective. A child sent to stand in the corner to think about the misbehavior that just occurred.

Start-Up Costs. Who knew you needed so much stuff to have a baby? It just starts with a nice bottle of wine and dinner.

Stock Split. When the kids' activities take them to different places. For instance, only one child gets to go to Grandma's at a time. A stock split can be beneficial if all the stocks have places to go. A stock split is not so great if one stock is left at home and none too happy about it.

Stop Order. Given when a child breaks away from your hand and runs towards the street. There are no negotiations. In panic, "Stop" is ordered and due to the tone and force of your voice, the child usually stops as quickly as he/she can physically gain back control of the little legs that have built up momentum.

Strike. What we don't allow our children to do.

Swing Shift. To be avoided, if possible. Trips to the park or backyard to use the swing set are great, but all that pushing back and forth can really wear a person out. While it does wonders to shape up the arms, you can only push for so long. Actually, the slide shift is easier. You just have to catch the kids at the bottom.

Take-Away. When you attend a child's birthday party, you can count on three things: Entertainment or games, something sweet and a goody bag (the take-away). When you host a child's birthday party, the take-away can be the real stumper. You want the kids to be happy with the contents, you want the parents to be happy with the contents, you want the kids' fond memories of the party to be reinforced with the goody bag, but you don't want to break the bank in putting them together. The importance (and difficulty) of coming up with a good take-away can't be overestimated.

Takeover Strategy. Your plot to get back control of the TV remote or computer from your children. "Time for bed." "Don't you have homework?"

Tender. Some children are just more sensitive than others. These are precious treasures and must be protected, yet encouraged to grow and become stronger.

Time Deposit. Reading to your children every night. Devoting complete attention to your child. Building something together. These investments will provide many dividends over the years.

Time Study. Does anyone even learn to tell time from an analog clock anymore? Or is it all digital?

Trade Policy. What you must establish with your children when they are old enough to trade Barbies, Hot Wheel cars, and the like with friends. When you are blessed with generous children, you can end up with a huge financial loss. A prized Hot Wheels car that has been in the family for two generations perhaps should not be traded for a piece of bubble gum.

Trickle-Down Theory. Method of becoming aware of an overflowing toilet or bathtub on the second floor of your house. When a plumbing disaster occurs upstairs and you only learn of it when you see the dripping of water from the ceiling onto furniture, and then, eventually, onto the floor on the first floor, you rue the day this theory was developed. See **Flow Chart** for being prepared for such a plumbing disaster.

Trust Fund. What you lovingly invest in those first few years of your child's life. Caring for them, feeding them, teaching them to feed themselves, being there during scary thunderstorms, teaching them the alphabet, helping them ride bicycles, buying them their first baseball gloves . . . what your teen can nearly deplete in one bad weekend.

Luckily, most kids start with a large trust fund. Some deductions may be taken throughout the years, but, hopefully, deposits are made periodically and the account continues to grow.

Turnover. Eventually this will happen to everything you put on your child's highchair tray — turned over, upside down, and then, often, actually hurled into the air.

Not All Carry-Ons Are Created Equal

It's among the harder decisions in life: What to carry on an airplane when you travel. Mindful of current regulations, many choices remain. For instance, those gold lamé party pants — always such crowd pleasers — can't possibly be packed, and to carry them on means bringing onboard almost nothing else. And, of course, there's Fido. Pocketsize, it just doesn't seem fair to leave him at home when you'll be off having so much fun. Then, there's no getting around it: The children must be considered.

Traveling for business only complicates matters. Personal items as well as professional ones must be evaluated. Perhaps listing the benefits or problems is just the ticket.

Consider, for instance, these possible carry-ons: A portable computer (laptop A) versus an 18-month-old child (laptop B). Which one to take . . . which one to take?

Laptop A — Need to turn off during take-off and landing; you don't want to interfere with the electronic equipment needed to fly the plane. You're free to sleep, read or just quietly look out the window.

Laptop B — Can't possibly turn off, especially during take-off and landing. Changes in air pressure can cause pain in children's ears, often prompting cries and, sometimes, screams. And never mind *looking* out the window with this carry-on. If the cries are loud enough, you and the inhabitants of the entire plane will want to stick your heads *out* of the windows.

Laptop A — Can fold up and put under the seat when tired of holding.

Laptop B — Loves to contort body and hide out under your seat. Must be watchful, however, as this laptop will put in its mouth everything it finds under your chair, including another passenger's three-week old gum and the toes of the person sitting behind you.

Laptop A — Accidents are usually contained. You can erase them and start fresh.

Laptop B — Accidents, hopefully, are contained and aren't too smelly. You just hightail it to a private area to fix. If it was contained — and you have needed supplies — you can start again, relatively fresh.

Laptop A — You hope your laptop doesn't contract a virus. Some data may be lost. However, if it does get a virus, likely it won't spread to you.

Laptop B — You hope your laptop doesn't contract a virus. Breakfast and lunch of laptop would likely be lost on you. Besides, if it does get a virus, very likely it will spread to you.

Laptop A — You must protect the integrity of your work, as other passengers peer over your shoulders at the information appearing on the screen of your laptop.

Laptop B — You must protect yourself as the laptop uses your body parts for a ladder, climbing to your shoulders and peering at other passengers, playing games of peek-a-boo, making silly faces and, sometimes, drooling on their work.

Laptop A — A slim, lightweight carrying case holds laptop and easy-to-pack accessories like DVDs, discs, chargers and cords.

Laptop B — Have to carry heavy, often squirming laptop plus big, bulky carrying case bulging with such necessities as diapers, wipes, pacifiers, food, drinks and toys.

Laptop A — You arrive at your meeting, fully prepared; you spent the entire trip working on your laptop.

Laptop B — You arrive at your meeting, not at all prepared; you spent the entire trip working with your laptop.

Laptop A — You're eager to show off your laptop's latest developments. You'll use them in your presentation. Everyone at the meeting will be so impressed.

Laptop B — You're eager to show off your laptop's latest developments, yet you won't take it to the meeting. While everyone would be duly impressed, your laptop might distract from your presentation.

Laptop A — Pretty handy to have around. Knows lots of games. You've spent a lot of time inputting information into laptop. Yet, you receive little satisfaction from relationship. Besides, it can't hug worth a darn. If it gets lost or stolen, replacement would be a hassle, but, hopefully, everything was backed up.

Laptop B — Usually requires substantial effort to have around. You've spent a lot of time inputting information into laptop. It does know lots of games and makes you laugh. You love spending time with this laptop. You've learned so much from each other. Its hugs are the greatest. Absolutely no backup. Could never be replaced if lost or stolen. And yes, you do want to travel with this carry-on as much as possible.

Definitions

U-Z

Umbrella Policy. The rule regarding where children are allowed to open rain-shielding contraptions. They are not to be opened in the house, and under no circumstances are they ever to be opened in the car while it is in motion. Unless, of course, someone left a window open and you are moving through a car wash.

Unappreciated Assets. Large hips can be very useful. Opening doors, holding doors open, balancing kids and groceries and laundry baskets. Not every one views my extensive assets with such appreciation.

Underemployed. Our dog. He's the only one in the house that is always eager to do more. Although, just like everyone else, he scatters when the vacuum comes out.

Underperforming Asset. The child that just doesn't seem to be applying himself/herself in the way he/she seems capable of.

Unfair Trade Balance. If one splits something (a piece of candy, the last doughnut), the other gets to choose. This is in order to prevent an unfair trade. Keeps the power balanced.

Unrealized Appreciation. I am sure that my children greatly appreciate everything I do for them, even if they forget to ever tell me. But, luckily, I am not bitter. ☺

Unrecaptured Asset. When the children think the fish need a vacation and put them in the toilet ("like a trip to the lake," they say). But when the fish accidentally get flushed, there is no way to get them back. Suddenly, the pets are on a permanent ocean cruise.

Unsecured Bond. Allowing your child go on that overnight field trip, but hoping your voice will still be in his/her head. "I think I'd better put some sunscreen on." "No, I'll pass on that soda. Is there any milk?" "Isn't it about time we get some shut-eye?"

Valuation of Long-Term Assets. Great appreciation of grandparents and others who have accumulated more than six decades of memories and experiences.

Value Added. When you put additional cash onto the money card you've given your child to take to camp, to college or just to the mall.

Visible Means of Support. Occurs when the unsightly lines from undergarments show through outer garments. While you're glad the support is there, most times, you just don't want to see it. *Antonym*: **No Visible Means of Support.**

Website. The corner of my family room where spiders gather — no matter how often they're cleaned away.

Whistle-Blower. Teacher in charge on the playground.

Year-Over-Year Growth Chart. Those pencil marks in the hall doorway showing your child's height as measured at the beginning of each school year. — While some years show more growth than others — never a downturn here!

Zero Economic Growth. Braces, school uniforms, sports, summer camps, singing lessons, violin lessons, laptops, iPhones, video games, bikes, skate boards, swing sets, educational vacations, college — there are many reasons for zero economic growth.

Zipper Clause. Who would have guessed that something like this has to be taught? Little boys are the worst. Some parents resort to scare tactics: "If you don't remember to zip your zipper when getting dressed or after using the restroom, next time you check, it might not be there. And I'm not talking about the zipper."

Life Can't Be All Business . . .
History Lessons Hit Home

We are trying to raise politically aware children. We want them to be good citizens. We are not pushing them toward a particular party affiliation, just to be aware of important events and contributions to society. And I think when a politician has a good message, if we apply it to everyday life, we will remember the messages better. For instance, the Kennedys have been an important part of our nation's history. And with all due respect to the original intent, a couple of their phrases have proven particularly useful at our house.

For instance, Robert Kennedy once said, "Some men see things as they are and say, 'Why?' I dream of things that never were and say, 'Why not?'"

I, for one, think he was referring to housework.

You see, I like a clean house as much as the next guy. The only problem is, that after all that dusting, scrubbing, vacuuming and polishing — well, after a few months, you have to do it all again.

So some may see my house and say, "Why?" While I see my house and say, "In my dreams . . . right now I have other things to do."

Then, there was JFK's famous quote. While he proclaimed, "Ask not what your country can do for you. Ask what you can do for your country." I apply the same principle around the house with the kids, with just a slight twist. "Ask not what your mother can do for you. Ask what you can do for your mother!"

Now, there's a call to action!

Political leaders must have had kids in mind

Other politicians have proven helpful around the house too. Considering that I do enjoy eating at home, most times I don't mind cooking dinner and like to try different recipes. However, there are some days . . . and on those days, when I don't think I can boil another pot of pasta, convincingly disguise eggplant or think of another way to prepare a chicken breast, I once again call upon a leader of our country. Proving that we can learn and benefit even from those politicians whose weaknesses have been exposed and may have fallen from grace, I go to the door, grab the keys, put both of my arms in the air, forming V's with the forefingers and middle fingers on each hand and turn to my children and husband, shouting, "I'm not a cook. I'm not a cook." It's the family's signal to grab their shoes. We're eating out. Mom needs a night off.

And, Martin Luther King Jr. — why, he was an inspiration to us all. Yet while he could see the big picture, my scope is slightly narrower. In fact, when my children were younger, I once told them: "I have a dream. That someday we will all walk together across the street holding hands. That no one will run ahead and barely miss being run over. That no one will lag behind and get tangled in traffic. Yes, I have a dream; that we can all walk hand-in-hand."

And several times when perusing the video store for a weekend rental, I have had to say to my children after repeated pleadings for a purchase, "Read my lips. No new video games." Former President George H.W. Bush had used the "Read my lips" phrase regarding taxes. In my circumstances, my children's requests were merely taxing.

Then, when Samuel Adams said that "Mankind are governed more by their feelings than by reason," he had to be referring to children.

And, what about Benjamin Franklin when he said, "To find out a girl's faults, praise her to her girl friends." I didn't know he spent his spare timing hanging out at the mall with teenage girls.

But I often find myself quoting him as my daughters leave for an evening out with their friends, "Think of these things, whence you came, where you are going, and to whom you must account."

The Take-Away/The Goody Bag

See **Take-Away**.
It seems like you can't go anywhere these days without getting a take-away. Everyone wants you to have a reminder of their event. Attend a business meeting and the presenters want you to leave with an idea, a plan or new knowledge (or maybe even a magnet for your refrigerator). Go to a child's birthday party, you'll also get a take-away — the goody bag — candy or toys all nicely packaged following the party theme.

Even charities often give donors something so they'll remember their act of kindness (in case the tax deduction isn't reminder enough). I know someone who won a car at a charity event and drove it home. I guess the charity organizers thought it was the best way to drive home the benefits of charitable giving.

I wanted a take-away for this book. And of course, it had to follow the theme — bringing home the business world. So, I thought the following observation might nicely wrap up things and give you a little something to take away.

Years ago, many corporate annual reports were much more lavish than they are today. Beautiful photography, elegant designs and creative text, in addition to financial results, were the norm. One year, as I was assembling a company's annual report, working long days alongside the many individuals involved in the project, a very senior executive turned to me and said (neither of us had children at the time):

"You know, I think putting together an annual report is a lot like having a baby:
- It takes several months to produce.
- You have to be careful what you put into it.
- Everyone has opinions on what should go into it and how it will turn out.
- You really want to give it your best.
- You sure hope when it's all over that you like it."

Well, I haven't seen that guy since I've had my children, and I hear he has had a few of his own. But, *now*, I think we would agree:

Having a baby is **NOTHING** like putting out an annual report.